DISCOVER!

EARTH AND SPACE SCIENCE

PROBES IN SPACE

Beth Irving

Enslow PUBLISHING

Please visit our website, www.enslow.com. For a free color catalog of all our high-quality books, call toll free 1-800-398-2504 or fax 1-877-980-4454.

Cataloging-in-Publication Data
Names: Irving, Beth.
Title: Probes in space / Beth Irving.
Description: Buffalo, NY : Enslow Publishing, 2027. | Series: Earth and space science | Includes glossary and index.
Identifiers: ISBN 9781978550292 (pbk.) | ISBN 9781978550308 (library bound) | ISBN 9781978550315 (ebook)
Subjects: LCSH: Space probes–Juvenile literature. | Space robotics–Juvenile literature. | Outer space–Exploration–Juvenile literature.
Classification: LCC TL795.3 I785 2027 | DDC 629.435–dc23

Published in 2027 by
Enslow Publishing
2544 Clinton Street
Buffalo, NY 14224

Designer: Claire Vanden Branden
Editor: Noah Riccardi

Photo Credits: Cover, p. 1 Nostalgia for Infinity/Shutterstock.com; p. 5 Elliptic Studio/Shutterstock.com; p. 7 Aunt Spray/Shutterstock.com; pp. 9, 15, 17 NASA Images; p. 11 Artsiom P./Shutterstock.com; p. 13 buradaki/Shutterstock.com; p. 19 Rawpixel.com/Shutterstock.com; p. 21 joshimerbin/Shutterstock.com.

Printed in China

CPSIA compliance information: Batch #QS27ENS: For further information contact Enslow Publishing, at 1-800-398-2504.

CONTENTS

BOLDFACE WORDS APPEAR IN THE GLOSSARY.

WHAT ARE SPACE PROBES?

Scientists are always trying to learn about faraway objects in outer space. People can't fly so far. So how do we learn? We send space probes.

Space probes are ships that travel through space. People don't fly on space probes. Probes gather information and send it back to Earth.

THE FIRST PROBES

The first ever space probe was called *Sputnik*. It was launched by the Soviet Union in 1957. *Sputnik* was able to send a radio signal back to Earth. It was the very first object that humans ever sent into **orbit**.

The United States sent *Mariner 2* to Venus in 1962. It was the first probe to study another planet.

In 1971, *Mariner 9* began to orbit Mars. It was the first space probe to orbit another planet!

Probes can also land on the **surface** of a planet. The first space probes to do this were *Viking 1* and *Viking 2*. They went into space in 1975, flew for almost a full year, then landed on Mars. Their job was to study the surface of the planet.

EXPLORING DEEP SPACE

Some space probes study the **outer planets**. In 1977, *Voyager 1* flew into space. It **explored** Jupiter and Saturn, then left our **solar system**.

Years later, *Voyager 1* is still flying. It is the farthest object people have ever launched from Earth. It has traveled over 15 billion miles (25 billion km) from our planet.

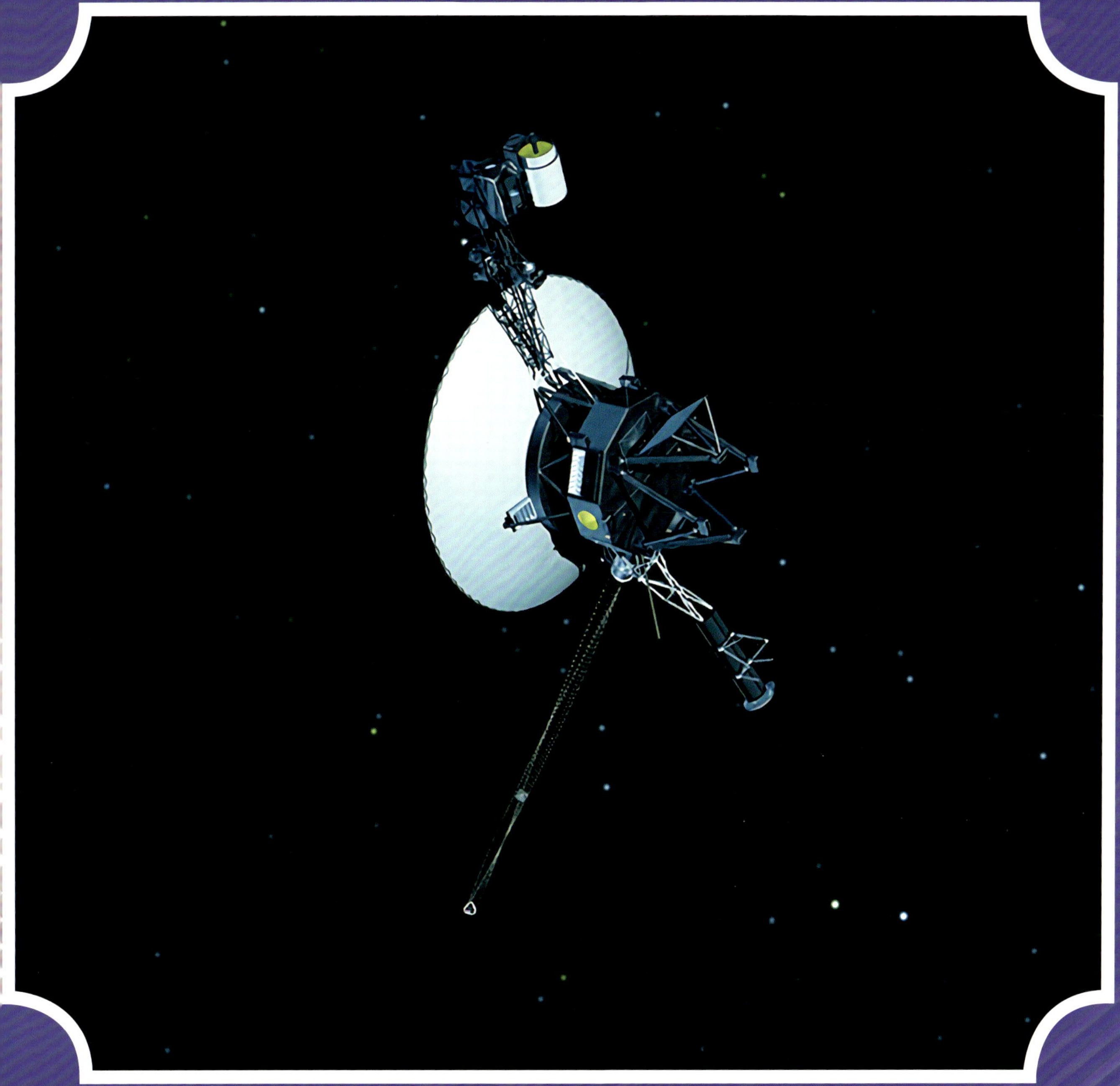

Pioneer 10 was the first probe to take photographs of Jupiter, in 1973. *Pioneer 11* studied Saturn. It flew past Saturn in 1979 and took pictures of the planet and its rings.

The first space probe to explore the planet Uranus was *Voyager 2* in 1986. In 1989, it visited Neptune, the last planet in our solar system. Then it flew into deep space. *Voyager 2* has flown over 13 billion miles (21 billion km) from Earth.

In 1997, the United States launched the *Cassini* space probe to Saturn. It was bigger than any probe built before it! *Cassini* was built to study Saturn in orbit around the planet.

Cassini arrived at Saturn in 2004. It studied Saturn's rings. It also looked at Saturn's many moons.

STUDYING MARS

Scientists want to learn as much as they can about Mars. Space probes help them do that. Many probes have been sent to orbit and even land on the planet.

Pathfinder was a space probe built to explore the surface of Mars. It landed on the planet in 1997. It helped scientists study rocks on Mars.

JPL

Pathfinder launched in 1996 and reached Mars in 1997. It carried a rover to the planet. This is a kind of robot that can move across the surface of a planet. The rover sent lots of pictures back to scientists on Earth.

The *Mars Odyssey* space probe began to orbit Mars in 2002. It searched for water on the planet. This probe found lots of ice on Mars.

THE FUTURE OF SPACEFLIGHT

In 2023, the *Jupiter Icy Moons Explorer (Juice)* launched from French Guiana. In the 2030s, it will send information to Earth about three of Jupiter's moons.

Space probes are still being sent out into space to help us learn more. They are very important tools for space explorers!

GLOSSARY

explored: Searched something to find out more about it.

outer planets: The planets of the solar system beyond the Asteroid Belt: Jupiter, Saturn, Uranus, and Neptune.

orbit: To move in a circle around something; also, the path of an object flying in a circle around something.

scientists: People who study the way things are and the way things work.

solar system: The sun and the objects in space that move around it.

surface: The outside layer of something.

FOR MORE INFORMATION

Books

Miller, Ron. *To the Stars: The Story of NASA*. Minneapolis, MN: Lerner Publications, 2025.

Wood, Alix. *Blast Off to Other Planets*. Buffalo, NY: Rosen Publishing, 2025.

Websites

Britannica Kids: Astronomy
kids.britannica.com/kids/article/astronomy/352798
Learn more about astronomy, the study of outer space.

NASA: Where Are Voyager 1 and 2 Now?
https://science.nasa.gov/mission/voyager/where-are-voyager-1-and-voyager-2-now/
See how far the Voyager probes have traveled at this site.

Publisher's note to educators and parents: Our editors have carefully reviewed these websites to ensure that they are suitable for students. Many websites change frequently, however, and we cannot guarantee that a site's future contents will continue to meet our high standards of quality and educational value. Be advised that students should be closely supervised whenever they access the internet.

INDEX